One, Two, Buckle My Shoe

Retold by Russell Punter

Illustrated by David Semple

One, two,

buckle my shoe.

Three, four,
knock at the door.

Five,
   six,

pick
up
sticks.

Seven, eight, lay them straight.

Nine, ten,

a big fat hen.

Eleven,
twelve,

dig and delve.

Thirteen, fourteen,
maids a-courting.

Fifteen,
sixteen,

maids in the kitchen.

Seventeen,
eighteen,

maids a-waiting.

Nineteen,
twenty,
my plate's empty.

Twenty-three,
twenty-four,

home once more.

Twenty-seven,
twenty-eight,
fasten the gate.

Twenty-nine, thirty,
"You're safe now, Gertie."

Edited by Jenny Tyler and Lesley Sims

First published in 2014 by Usborne Publishing Ltd., Usborne House, 83-85 Saffron Hill,
London EC1N 8RT, England. www.usborne.com Copyright © 2014 Usborne Publishing Ltd.